# A Christmas Carmen
## By John Greenleaf Whittier

# A Christmas Carmen,
# by John Greenleaf Whittier

I.
Sound over all waters, reach out from all lands,
The chorus of voices, the clasping of hands;
Sing hymns that were sung by the stars of the morn,
Sing songs of the angels when Jesus was born!
With glad jubilations
Bring hope to the nations!
The dark night is ending and dawn has begun:
Rise, hope of the ages, arise like the sun,
All speech flow to music, all hearts beat as one!

II.
Sing the bridal of nations! with chorals of love
Sing out the war-vulture and sing in the dove,
Till the hearts of the peoples keep time in accord,
And the voice of the world is the voice of the Lord!
Clasp hands of the nations
In strong gratulations:
The dark night is ending and dawn has begun;
Rise, hope of the ages, arise like the sun,
All speech flow to music, all hearts beat as one!

III.
Blow, bugles of battle, the marches of peace;
East, west, north, and south let the long quarrel cease
Sing the song of great joy that the angels began,
Sing of glory to God and of good-will to man!
Hark! joining in chorus
The heavens bend o'er us!
The dark night is ending and dawn has begun;
Rise, hope of the ages, arise like the sun,
All speech flow to music, all hearts beat as one!

# A Dream Of Summer,
# by John Greenleaf Whittier

Bland as the morning breath of June
The southwest breezes play;
And, through its haze, the winter noon
Seems warm as summer's day.

The snow-plumed Angel of the North
Has dropped his icy spear;
Again the mossy earth looks forth,
Again the streams gush clear.

The fox his hillside cell forsakes,
The muskrat leaves his nook,
The bluebird in the meadow brakes
Is singing with the brook.
'Bear up, O Mother Nature!' cry
Bird, breeze, and streamlet free;
'Our winter voices prophesy
Of summer days to thee!'

So, in those winters of the soul,
By bitter blasts and drear
O'erswept from Memory's frozen pole,
Will sunny days appear.
Reviving Hope and Faith, they show
The soul its living powers,
And how beneath the winter's snow
Lie germs of summer flowers!

The Night is mother of the Day,
The Winter of the Spring,
And ever upon old Decay
The greenest mosses cling.
Behind the cloud the starlight lurks,
Through showers the sunbeams fall;
For God, who loveth all His works,
Has left His hope with all!

# A Lament, by John Greenleaf Whittier

The circle is broken, one seat is forsaken,
One bud from the tree of our friendship is shaken;
One heart from among us no longer shall thrill
With joy in our gladness, or grief in our ill.

Weep! lonely and lowly are slumbering now
The light of her glances, the pride of her brow;
Weep! sadly and long shall we listen in vain
To hear the soft tones of her welcome again.

Give our tears to the dead! For humanity's claim
From its silence and darkness is ever the same;

The hope of that world whose existence is bliss
May not stifle the tears of the mourners of this.

For, oh! if one glance the freed spirit can throw
On the scene of its troubled probation below,
Than the pride of the marble, the pomp of the dead,
To that glance will be dearer the tears which we shed.

Oh, who can forget the mild light of her smile,
Over lips moved with music and feeling the while,
The eye's deep enchantment, dark, dream-like, and clear,
In the glow of its gladness, the shade of its tear.

And the charm of her features, while over the whole
Played the hues of the heart and the sunshine of soul;
And the tones of her voice, like the music which seems
Murmured low in our ears by the Angel of dreams!

But holier and dearer our memories hold
Those treasures of feeling, more precious than gold,
The love and the kindness and pity which gave
Fresh flowers for the bridal, green wreaths for the grave!

The heart ever open to Charity's claim,
Unmoved from its purpose by censure and blame,
While vainly alike on her eye and her ear
Fell the scorn of the heartless, the jesting and jeer.

How true to our hearts was that beautiful sleeper
With smiles for the joyful, with tears for the weeper,
Yet, evermore prompt, whether mournful or gay,
With warnings in love to the passing astray.

For, though spotless herself, she could sorrow for them
Who sullied with evil the spirit's pure gem;
And a sigh or a tear could the erring reprove,
And the sting of reproof was still tempered by love.

As a cloud of the sunset, slow melting in heaven,
As a star that is lost when the daylight is given,
As a glad dream of slumber, which wakens in bliss,
She hath passed to the world of the holy from this.

# A Legacy, by John Greenleaf Whittier

Friend of my many years!
When the great silence falls, at last, on me,
Let me not leave, to pain and sadden thee,
A memory of tears,
But pleasant thoughts alone.
Of one who was thy friendship's honored guest
And drank the wine of consolation pressed
From sorrows of thy own.
I leave with thee a sense
Of hands upheld and trials rendered less,
The unselfish joy which is to helpfulness
Its own great recompense.
The knowledge that from thine,
As from the garments of the Master, stole
Calmness and strength, the virtue which makes whole
And heals without a sign.
Yea more, the assurance strong
That love, which fails of perfect utterance here,
Lives on to fill the heavenly atmosphere
With its immortal song.

# A Memorial, by John Greenleaf Whittier

Oh, thicker, deeper, darker growing,
The solemn vista to the tomb
Must know henceforth another shadow,
And give another cypress room.

In love surpassing that of brothers,
We walked, O friend, from childhood's day;
And, looking back o'er fifty summers,
Our footprints track a common way.

One in our faith, and one our longing
To make the world within our reach
Somewhat the better for our living,
And gladder for our human speech.

Thou heard'st with me the far-off voices,
The old beguiling song of fame,
But life to thee was warm and present,
And love was better than a name.

To homely joys and loves and friendships

Thy genial nature fondly clung;
And so the shadow on the dial
Ran back and left thee always young.

And who could blame the generous weakness
Which, only to thyself unjust,
So overprized the worth of others,
And dwarfed thy own with self-distrust?

All hearts grew warmer in the presence
Of one who, seeking not his own,
Gave freely for the love of giving,
Nor reaped for self the harvest sown.

Thy greeting smile was pledge and prelude
Of generous deeds and kindly words;
In thy large heart were fair guest-chambers,
Open to sunrise and the birds;

The task was thine to mould and fashion
Life's plastic newness into grace
To make the boyish heart heroic,
And light with thought the maiden's face.

O'er all the land, in town and prairie,
With bended heads of mourning, stand
The living forms that owe their beauty
And fitness to thy shaping hand.

Thy call has come in ripened manhood,
The noonday calm of heart and mind,
While I, who dreamed of thy remaining
To mourn me, linger still behind,

Live on, to own, with self-upbraiding,
A debt of love still due from me,--
The vain remembrance of occasions,
Forever lost, of serving thee.

It was not mine among thy kindred
To join the silent funeral prayers,
But all that long sad day of summer
My tears of mourning dropped with theirs.

All day the sea-waves sobbed with sorrow,
The birds forgot their merry trills
All day I heard the pines lamenting
With thine upon thy homestead hills.

Green be those hillside pines forever,
And green the meadowy lowlands be,
And green the old memorial beeches,
Name-carven in the woods of Lee.

Still let them greet thy life companions
Who thither turn their pilgrim feet,
In every mossy line recalling
A tender memory sadly sweet.

O friend! if thought and sense avail not
To know thee henceforth as thou art,
That all is well with thee forever
I trust the instincts of my heart.

Thine be the quiet habitations,
Thine the green pastures, blossom-sown,
And smiles of saintly recognition,
As sweet and tender as thy own.

Thou com'st not from the hush and shadow
To meet us, but to thee we come,
With thee we never can be strangers,
And where thou art must still be home.

# A Mystery, by John Greenleaf Whittier

The river hemmed with leaning trees
Wound through its meadows green;
A low, blue line of mountains showed
The open pines between.

One sharp, tall peak above them all
Clear into sunlight sprang
I saw the river of my dreams,
The mountains that I sang!

No clue of memory led me on,
But well the ways I knew;
A feeling of familiar things
With every footstep grew.

Not otherwise above its crag
Could lean the blasted pine;
Not otherwise the maple hold

Aloft its red ensign.

So up the long and shorn foot-hills
The mountain road should creep;
So, green and low, the meadow fold
Its red-haired kine asleep.

The river wound as it should wind;
Their place the mountains took;
The white torn fringes of their clouds
Wore no unwonted look.

Yet ne'er before that river's rim
Was pressed by feet of mine,
Never before mine eyes had crossed
That broken mountain line.

A presence, strange at once and known,
Walked with me as my guide;
The skirts of some forgotten life
Trailed noiseless at my side.

Was it a dim-remembered dream?
Or glimpse through ions old?
The secret which the mountains kept
The river never told.

But from the vision ere it passed
A tender hope I drew,
And, pleasant as a dawn of spring,
The thought within me grew,

That love would temper every change,
And soften all surprise,
And, misty with the dreams of earth,
The hills of Heaven arise.

# The Frost Spirit
## By
## John Greenleaf Whittier

# THE FROST SPIRIT

He comes, he comes, the Frost Spirit comes
You may trace his footsteps now
On the naked woods and the blasted fields and the
brown hill's withered brow.
He has smitten the leaves of the gray old trees
where their pleasant green came forth,
And the winds, which follow wherever he goes,
have shaken them down to earth.

He comes, he comes, the Frost Spirit comes!
from the frozen Labrador,
From the icy bridge of the Northern seas, which
the white bear wanders o'er,
Where the fisherman's sail is stiff with ice, and the
luckless forms below
In the sunless cold of the lingering night into
marble statues grow

He comes, he comes, the Frost Spirit comes
on the rushing Northern blast,
And the dark Norwegian pines have bowed as his
fearful breath went past.
With an unscorched wing he has hurried on,
where the fires of Hecla glow
On the darkly beautiful sky above and the ancient
ice below.

He comes, he comes, the Frost Spirit comes
and the quiet lake shall feel
The torpid touch of his glazing breath, and ring to
the skater's heel;
And the streams which danced on the broken
rocks, or sang to the leaning grass,
Shall bow again to their winter chain, and in
mournful silence pass.
He comes, he comes, the Frost Spirit comes!
Let us meet him as we may,
And turn with the light of the parlorfire his evil
power away;

And gather closer the circle round, when that
firelight dances high,
And laugh at the shriek of the baffled Fiend as
his sounding wing goes by!

## THE MERRIMAC

"The Indians speak of a beautiful river, far to the south,
which they call Merrimac." SIEUR. DE MONTS,    .
Stream of my fathers! sweetly still
The sunset rays thy valley fill;

Poured slantwise down the long defile,
Wave, wood, and spire beneath them smile.
I see the winding Powow fold

The green hill in its belt of gold,
And following down its wavy line,
Its sparkling waters blend with thine.
There's not a tree upon thy side,

Nor rock, which thy returning tide
As yet hath left abrupt and stark
Above thy evening watermark;

No calm cove with its rocky hem,
No isle whose emerald swells begin
Thy broad, smooth current; not a sail
Bowed to the freshening ocean gale;
No small boat with its busy oars,

Nor gray wall sloping to thy shores;
Nor farmhouse with its maple shade,
Or rigid poplar colonnade,

But lies distinct and full in sight,
Beneath this gush of sunset light.
Centuries ago, that harborbar,
Stretching its length of foam afar,
And Salisbury's beach of shining sand,
And yonder island's wavesmoothed strand,

Saw the adventurer's tiny sail,

Flit, stooping from the eastern gale;
And o'er these woods and waters broke
The cheer from Britain's hearts of oak,
As brightly on the voyager's eye,
Weary of forest, sea, and sky,

Breaking the dull continuous wood,
The Merrimac rolled down his flood;
Mingling that clear pellucid brook,
Which channels vast Agioochook

When springtime's sun and shower unlock
The frozen fountains of the rock,
And more abundant waters given
From that pure lake, "The Smile of Heaven,"
Tributes from vale and mountainside,
With ocean's dark, eternal tide!

On yonder rocky cape, which braves
The stormy challenge of the waves,
Midst tangled vine and dwarfish wood,
The hardy AngloSaxon stood,

Planting upon the topmost crag
The staff of England's battleflag;
And, while from out its heavy fold
Saint George's crimson cross unrolled,
Midst roll of drum and trumpet blare,
And weapons brandishing in air,

He gave to that lone promontory
The sweetest name in all his story;
Of her, the flower of Islam's daughters,
Whose harems look on Stamboul's waters,
Who, when the chance of war had bound
The Moslem chain his limbs around,
Wreathed o'er with silk that iron chain,
Soothed with her smiles his hours of pain,
And fondly to her youthful slave

A dearer gift than freedom gave.

But look! the yellow light no more
Streams down on wave and verdant shore;
And clearly on the calm air swells
The twilight voice of distant bells.

From Ocean's bosom, white and thin,
The mists come slowly rolling in;
Hills, woods, the river's rocky rim,
Amidst the sea like vapor swim,

While yonder lonely coastlight, set
Within its wavewashed minaret,
Half quenched, a beamless star and pale,
Shines dimly through its cloudy veil!

Home of my fathers! I have stood
Where Hudson rolled his lordly flood
Seen sunrise rest and sunset fade
Along his frowning Palisade;

Looked down the Appalachian peak
On Juniata's silver streak;
Have seen along his valley gleam
The Mohawk's softly winding stream;
The level light of sunset shine

Through broad Potomac's hem of pine;
And autumn's rainbowtinted banner
Hang lightly o'er the Susquehanna;
Yet wheresoe'er his step might be,

Thy wandering child looked back to thee!
Heard in his dreams thy river's sound
Of murmuring on its pebbly bound,
The unforgotten swell and roar
Of waves on thy familiar shore;
And saw, amidst the curtained gloom
And quiet of his lonely room,

Thy sunset scenes before him pass;
As, in Agrippa's magic glass,
The loved and lost arose to view,

Remembered groves in greenness grew,
Bathed still in childhood's morning dew,
Along whose bowers of beauty swept
Whatever Memory's mourners wept,
Sweet faces, which the charnel kept,

Young, gentle eyes, which long had slept;
And while the gazer leaned to trace,
More near, some dear familiar face,
He wept to find the vision flown,
A phantom and a dream alone!

## HAMPTON BEACH

The sunlight glitters keen and bright,
Where, miles away,
Lies stretching to my dazzled sight
A luminous belt, a misty light,
Beyond the dark pine bluffs and wastes of sandy gray.

The tremulous shadow of the Sea!
Against its ground
Of silvery light, rock, hill, and tree,
Still as a picture, clear and free,
With varying outline mark the coast for miles around.

On on we tread with looseflung rein
Our seaward way,
Through darkgreen fields and blossoming grain,
Where the wild brierrose skirts the lane,
And bends above our heads the flowering locust spray.

Ha! like a kind hand on my brow
Comes this fresh breeze,
Cooling its dull and feverish glow,
While through my being seems to flow
The breath of a new life, the healing of the seas!

Now rest we, where this grassy mound
His feet hath set
In the great waters, which have bound
His granite ankles greenly round
With long and tangled moss, and weeds with cool spray wet.

Goodby to Pain and Care! I take
Mine ease today
Here where these sunny waters break,
And ripples this keen breeze, I shake
All burdens from the heart, all weary thoughts away.

I draw a freer breath, I seem
Like all I see
Waves in the sun, the whitewinged gleam
Of seabirds in the slanting beam,
And faroff sails which flit before the southwind free.

So when Time's veil shall fall asunder,
The soul may know
No fearful change, nor sudden wonder,
Nor sink the weight of mystery under,
But with the upward rise, and with the vastness grow.

And all we shrink from now may seem
No new revealing;
Familiar as our childhood's stream,
Or pleasant memory of a dream
The loved and cherished Past upon the new life stealing.

Serene and mild the untried light
May have its dawning;
And, as in summer's northern night
The evening and the dawn unite,
The sunset hues of Time blend with the soul's new morning.

I sit alone; in foam and spray
Wave after wave
Breaks on the rocks which, stern and gray,
Shoulder the broken tide away,

Or murmurs hoarse and strong through mossy cleft and cave.

What heed I of the dusty land
And noisy town?
I see the mighty deep expand
From its white line of glimmering sand
To where the blue of heaven on bluer waves shuts down!

In listless quietude of mind,
I yield to all
The change of cloud and wave and wind
And passive on the flood reclined,
I wander with the waves, and with them rise and fall.

But look, thou dreamer! wave and shore
In shadow lie;
The nightwind warns me back once more
To where, my native hilltops o'er,
Bends like an arch of fire the glowing sunset sky.

So then, beach, bluff, and wave, farewell!
I bear with me
No token stone nor glittering shell,
But long and oft shall Memory tell
Of this brief thoughtful hour of musing by the Sea.

## A DREAM OF SUMMER.

Bland as the morning breath of June
The southwest breezes play;
And, through its haze, the winter noon
Seems warm as summer's day.
The snowplumed Angel of the North
Has dropped his icy spear;
Again the mossy earth looks forth,
Again the streams gush clear.

The fox his hillside cell forsakes,
The muskrat leaves his nook,
The bluebird in the meadow brakes
Is singing with the brook.

"Bear up, O Mother Nature!" cry
Bird, breeze, and streamlet free;
"Our winter voices prophesy
Of summer days to thee!"

So, in those winters of the soul,
By bitter blasts and drear
O'erswept from Memory's frozen pole,
Will sunny days appear.
Reviving Hope and Faith, they show
The soul its living powers,
And how beneath the winter's snow
Lie germs of summer flowers!

The Night is mother of the Day,
The Winter of the Spring,
And ever upon old Decay
The greenest mosses cling.
Behind the cloud the starlight lurks,
Through showers the sunbeams fall;
For God, who loveth all His works,
Has left His hope with all!

## THE LAKESIDE

The shadows round the inland sea
Are deepening into night;
Slow up the slopes of Ossipee
They chase the lessening light.
Tired of the long day's blinding heat,
I rest my languid eye,
Lake of the Hills! where, cool and sweet,
Thy sunset waters lie!

Along the sky, in wavy lines,
O'er isle and reach and bay,
Greenbelted with eternal pines,
The mountains stretch away.
Below, the maple masses sleep
Where shore with water blends,
While midway on the tranquil deep

The evening light descends.

So seemed it when yon hill's red crown,
Of old, the Indian trod,
And, through the sunset air, looked down
Upon the Smile of God.
To him of light and shade the laws
No forest skeptic taught;
Their living and eternal Cause
His truer instinct sought.

He saw these mountains in the light
Which now across them shines;
This lake, in summer sunset bright,
Walled round with sombering pines.
God near him seemed; from earth and skies
His loving voice he beard,
As, face to face, in Paradise,
Man stood before the Lord.

Thanks, O our Father! that, like him,
Thy tender love I see,
In radiant hill and woodland dim,
And tinted sunset sea.
For not in mockery dost Thou fill
Our earth with light and grace;
Thou hid'st no dark and cruel will
Behind Thy smiling face!

## AUTUMN THOUGHTS

Gone hath the Spring, with all its flowers,
And gone the Summer's pomp and show,
And Autumn, in his leafless bowers,
Is waiting for the Winter's snow.

I said to Earth, so cold and gray,
"An emblem of myself thou art."
"Not so," the Earth did seem to say,
"For Spring shall warm my frozen heart."
I soothe my wintry sleep with dreams

Of warmer sun and softer rain,
And wait to hear the sound of streams
And songs of merry birds again.

But thou, from whom the Spring hath gone,
For whom the flowers no longer blow,
Who standest blighted and forlorn,
Like Autumn waiting for the snow;

No hope is thine of sunnier hours,
Thy Winter shall no more depart;
No Spring revive thy wasted flowers,
Nor Summer warm thy frozen heart.

## ON RECEIVING AN EAGLE'S QUILL FROM LAKE SUPERIOR.

All day the darkness and the cold
Upon my heart have lain,
Like shadows on the winter sky,
Like frost upon the pane;

But now my torpid fancy wakes,
And, on thy Eagle's plume,
Rides forth, like Sindbad on his bird,
Or witch upon her broom!

Below me roar the rocking pines,
Before me spreads the lake
Whose long and solemnsounding waves
Against the sunset break.

I hear the wild RiceEater thresh
The grain he has not sown;
I see, with flashing scythe of fire,
The prairie harvest mown!

I hear the faroff voyager's horn;
I see the Yankee's trail,
His foot on every mountainpass,
On every stream his sail.

By forest, lake, and waterfall,
I see his pedler show;
The mighty mingling with the mean,
The lofty with the low.

He's whittling by St. Mary's Falls,
Upon his loaded wain;
He's measuring o'er the Pictured Rocks,
With eager eyes of gain.

I hear the mattock in the mine,
The axestroke in the dell,
The clamor from the Indian lodge,
The Jesuit chapel bell!

I see the swarthy trappers come
From Mississippi's springs;
And warchiefs with their painted brows,
And crests of eagle wings.

Behind the scared squaw's birch canoe,
The steamer smokes and raves;
And city lots are staked for sale
Above old Indian graves.

I hear the tread of pioneers
Of nations yet to be;
The first low wash of waves, where soon
Shall roll a human sea.

The rudiments of empire here
Are plastic yet and warm;
The chaos of a mighty world
Is rounding into form!

Each rude and jostling fragment soon
Its fitting place shall find,
The raw material of a State,
Its muscle and its mind!

And, westering still, the star which leads

The New World in its train
Has tipped with fire the icy spears
Of many a mountain chain.

The snowy cones of Oregon
Are kindling on its way;
And California's golden sands
Gleam brighter in its ray!

Then blessings on thy eagle quill,
As, wandering far and wide,
I thank thee for this twilight dream
And Fancy's airy ride!

Yet, welcomer than regal plumes,
Which Western trappers find,
Thy free and pleasant thoughts, chance sown,
Like feathers on the wind.

Thy symbol be the mountainbird,
Whose glistening quill I hold;
Thy home the ample air of hope,
And memory's sunset gold!

In thee, let joy with duty join,
And strength unite with love,
The eagle's pinions folding round
The warm heart of the dove!

So, when in darkness sleeps the vale
Where still the blind bird clings
The sunshine of the upper sky
Shall glitter on thy wings!

## APRIL.

"The spring comes slowly up this way."
Christabel.
'T is the noon of the springtime, yet never a bird
In the windshaken elm or the maple is heard;
For green meadowgrasses wide levels of snow,

And blowing of drifts where the crocus should blow;

Where windflower and violet, amber and white,
On southsloping brooksides should smile in the light,
O'er the cold winterbeds of their latewaking roots
The frosty flake eddies, the icecrystal shoots;
And, longing for light, under winddriven heaps,
Round the boles of the pinewood the groundlaurel creeps,

Unkissed of the sunshine, unbaptized of showers,
With buds scarcely swelled, which should burst into flowers
We wait for thy coming, sweet wind of the south!
For the touch of thy light wings, the kiss of thy mouth;
For the yearly evangel thou bearest from God,
Resurrection and life to the graves of the sod!

Up our long rivervalley, for days, have not ceased
The wail and the shriek of the bitter northeast,
Raw and chill, as if winnowed through ices and snow,
All the way from the land of the wild Esquimau,
Until all our dreams of the land of the blest,

Like that red hunter's, turn to the sunny southwest.
O soul of the springtime, its light and its breath,
Bring warmth to this coldness, bring life to this death;
Renew the great miracle; let us behold
The stone from the mouth of the sepulchre rolled,
And Nature, like Lazarus, rise, as of old!

Let our faith, which in darkness and coldness has lain,
Revive with the warmth and the brightness again,
And in blooming of flower and budding of tree
The symbols and types of our destiny see;

The life of the springtime, the life of the whole,
And, as sun to the sleeping earth, love to the soul!

**PICTURES**

**I.**

Light, warmth, and sprouting greenness, and o'er all
Blue, stainless, steelbright ether, raining down
Tranquillity upon the deephushed town,
The freshening meadows, and the hillsides brown;
Voice of the westwind from the hills of pine,
And the brimmed river from its distant fall,
Low hum of bees, and joyous interlude
Of birdsongs in the streamletskirting wood,
Heralds and prophecies of sound and sight,
Blessed forerunners of the warmth and light,
Attendant angels to the house of prayer,
With reverent footsteps keeping pace with mine,
Once more, through God's great love, with you I share
A morn of resurrection sweet and fair
As that which saw, of old, in Palestine,
Immortal Love uprising in fresh bloom
From the dark night and winter of the tomb!

## II.

White with its sunbleached dust, the pathway winds
Before me; dust is on the shrunken grass,
And on the trees beneath whose boughs I pass;
Frail screen against the Hunter of the sky,
Who, glaring on me with his lidless eye,

While mounting with his dogstar high and higher
Ambushed in light intolerable, unbinds
The burnished quiver of his shafts of fire.
Between me and the hot fields of his South
A tremulous glow, as from a furnacemouth,
Glimmers and swims before my dazzled sight,
As if the burning arrows of his ire

Broke as they fell, and shattered into light;
Yet on my cheek I feel the western wind,
And hear it telling to the orchard trees,
And to the faint and flowerforsaken bees,
Tales of fair meadows, green with constant streams,
And mountains rising blue and cool behind,
Where in moist dells the purple orchis gleams,

And starred with white the virgin's bower is twined.
So the o'erwearied pilgrim, as he fares

Along life's summer waste, at times is fanned,
Even at noontide, by the cool, sweet airs
Of a serener and a holier land,

Fresh as the morn, and as the dewfall bland.
Breath of the blessed Heaven for which we pray,
Blow from the eternal hills! make glad our earthly way!

## SUMMER BY THE LAKESIDE

## LAKE WINNIPESAUKEE.

### I. NOON.

White clouds, whose shadows haunt the deep,
Light mists, whose soft embraces keep
The sunshine on the hills asleep!

O isles of calm! O dark, still wood!
And stiller skies that overbrood
Your rest with deeper quietude!

O shapes and hues, dim beckoning, through
Yon mountain gaps, my longing view
Beyond the purple and the blue,

To stiller sea and greener land,
And softer lights and airs more bland,
And skies, the hollow of God's hand!

Transfused through you, O mountain friends!
With mine your solemn spirit blends,
And life no more hath separate ends.

I read each misty mountain sign,
I know the voice of wave and pine,
And I am yours, and ye are mine.

Life's burdens fall, its discords cease,
I lapse into the glad release
Of Nature's own exceeding peace.

O welcome calm of heart and mind!
As falls yon firtree's loosened rind
To leave a tenderer growth behind,

So fall the weary years away;
A child again, my head I lay
Upon the lap of this sweet day.

This western wind hath Lethean powers,
Yon noonday cloud nepenthe showers,
The lake is white with lotusflowers!

Even Duty's voice is faint and low,
And slumberous Conscience, waking slow,
Forgets her blotted scroll to show.

The Shadow which pursues us all,
Whose evernearing steps appall,
Whose voice we hear behind us call,

That Shadow blends with mountain gray,
It speaks but what the light waves say,
Death walks apart from Fear today!

Rocked on her breast, these pines and I
Alike on Nature's love rely;
And equal seems to live or die.

Assured that He whose presence fills
With light the spaces of these hills
No evil to His creatures wills,

The simple faith remains, that He
Will do, whatever that may be,
The best alike for man and tree.

What mosses over one shall grow,

What light and life the other know,
Unanxious, leaving Him to show.

## II. EVENING.

Yon mountain's side is black with night,
While, broadorhed, o'er its gleaming crown
The moon, slowrounding into sight,
On the hushed inland sea looks down.

How start to light the clustering isles,
Each silverhemmed! How sharply show
The shadows of their rocky piles,
And treetops in the wave below!

How far and strange the mountains seem,
Dimlooming through the pale, still light
The vague, vast grouping of a dream,
They stretch into the solemn night.

Beneath, lake, wood, and peopled vale,
Hushed by that presence grand and grave,
Are silent, save the cricket's wail,
And low response of leaf and wave.

Fair scenes! whereto the Day and Night
Make rival love, I leave ye soon,
What time before the eastern light
The pale ghost of the setting moon

Shall hide behind yon rocky spines,
And the young archer, Morn, shall break
His arrows on the mountain pines,
And, goldensandalled, walk the lake!

Farewell! around this smiling bay
Gayhearted Health, and Life in bloom,
With lighter steps than mine, may stray
In radiant summers yet to come.

But none shall more regretful leave

These waters and these hills than I
Or, distant, fonder dream how eve
Or dawn is painting wave and sky;

How rising moons shine sad and mild
On wooded isle and silvering bay;
Or setting suns beyond the piled
And purple mountains lead the day;

Nor laughing girl, nor bearding boy,
Nor fullpulsed manhood, lingering here,
Shall add, to life's abounding joy,
The charmed repose to suffering dear.

Still waits kind Nature to impart
Her choicest gifts to such as gain
An entrance to her loving heart
Through the sharp discipline of pain.

Forever from the Hand that takes
One blessing from us others fall;
And, soon or late, our Father makes
His perfect recompense to all!

Oh, watched by Silence and the Night,
And folded in the strong embrace
Of the great mountains, with the light
Of the sweet heavens upon thy face,

Lake of the Northland! keep thy dower
Of beauty still, and while above
Thy solemn mountains speak of power,
Be thou the mirror of God's love.

## THE FRUITGIFT.

Last night, just as the tints of autumn's sky
Of sunset faded from our hills and streams,
I sat, vague listening, lapped in twilight dreams,
To the leaf's rustle, and the cricket's cry.

Then, like that basket, flush with summer fruit,
Dropped by the angels at the Prophet's foot,
Came, unannounced, a gift of clustered sweetness,
Fullorbed, and glowing with the prisoned beams
Of summery suns, and rounded to completeness
By kisses of the southwind and the dew.
Thrilled with a glad surprise, methought I knew
The pleasure of the homewardturning Jew,
When Eshcol's clusters on his shoulders lay,
Dropping their sweetness on his desert way.

I said, "This fruit beseems no world of sin.
Its parent vine, rooted in Paradise,
O'ercrept the wall, and never paid the price
Of the great mischief, an ambrosial tree,
Eden's exotic, somehow smuggled in,
To keep the thorns and thistles company."
Perchance our frail, sad mother plucked in haste
A single vineslip as she passed the gate,
Where the dread sword alternate paled and burned,
And the stern angel, pitying her fate,
Forgave the lovely trespasser, and turned
Aside his face of fire; and thus the waste
And fallen world hath yet its annual taste
Of primal good, to prove of sin the cost,
And show by one gleaned ear the mighty harvest lost.

.

# FLOWERS IN WINTER

## PAINTED UPON A PORTE LIVRE.

How strange to greet, this frosty morn,
In graceful counterfeit of flowers,
These children of the meadows, born
Of sunshine and of showers!

How well the conscious wood retains
The pictures of its flowersown home,
The lights and shades, the purple stains,
And golden hues of bloom!

It was a happy thought to bring
To the dark season's frost and rime
This painted memory of spring,
This dream of summertime.

Our hearts are lighter for its sake,
Our fancy's age renews its youth,
And dimremembered fictions take
The guise of present truth.

A wizard of the Merrimac,
So old ancestral legends say,
Could call green leaf and blossom back
To frosted stem and spray.

The dry logs of the cottage wall,
Beneath his touch, put out their leaves
The claybound swallow, at his call,
Played round the icy eaves.

The settler saw his oaken flail
Take bud, and bloom before his eyes;
From frozen pools he saw the pale,
Sweet summer lilies rise.

To their old homes, by man profaned,
Came the sad dryads, exiled long,

And through their leafy tongues complained
Of household use and wrong.

The beechen platter sprouted wild,
The pipkin wore its oldtime green
The cradle o'er the sleeping child
Became a leafy screen.

Haply our gentle friend hath met,
While wandering in her sylvan quest,
Haunting his native woodlands yet,
That Druid of the West;

And, while the dew on leaf and flower
Glistened in moonlight clear and still,
Learned the dusk wizard's spell of power,
And caught his trick of skill.

But welcome, be it new or old,
The gift which makes the day more bright,
And paints, upon the ground of cold
And darkness, warmth and light.

Without is neither gold nor green;
Within, for birds, the birchlogs sing;
Yet, summerlike, we sit between
The autumn and the spring.

The one, with bridal blush of rose,
And sweetest breath of woodland balm,
And one whose matron lips unclose
In smiles of saintly calm.

Fill soft and deep, O winter snow!
The sweet azalea's oaken dells,
And hide the bank where roses blow,
And swing the azure bells!

O'erlay the amber violet's leaves,
The purple aster's brookside home,
Guard all the flowers her pencil gives

A life beyond their bloom.

And she, when spring comes round again,
By greening slope and singing flood
Shall wander, seeking, not in vain,
Her darlings of the wood.

## THE MAYFLOWERS

The trailing arbutus, or mayflower, grows abundantly in the vicinity of Plymouth, and was the first flower that greeted the Pilgrims after their fearful winter. The name mayflower was familiar in England, as the application of it to the historic vessel shows, but it was applied by the English, and still is, to the hawthorn. Its use in New England in connection with Epigma repens dates from a very early day, some claiming that the first Pilgrims so used it, in affectionate memory of the vessel and its English flower association.

Sad Mayflower! watched by winter stars,
And nursed by winter gales,
With petals of the sleeted spars,
And leaves of frozen sails!

What had she in those dreary hours,
Within her icerimmed bay,
In common with the wildwood flowers,
The first sweet smiles of May?

Yet, "God be praised!" the Pilgrim said,
Who saw the blossoms peer
Above the brown leaves, dry and dead,
"Behold our Mayflower here!"

"God wills it: here our rest shall be,
Our years of wandering o'er;
For us the Mayflower of the sea
Shall spread her sails no more."

O sacred flowers of faith and hope,
As sweetly now as then
Ye bloom on many a birchen slope,
In many a pinedark glen.

Behind the seawall's rugged length,
Unchanged, your leaves unfold,
Like love behind the manly strength
Of the brave hearts of old.

So live the fathers in their sons,
Their sturdy faith be ours,
And ours the love that overruns
Its rocky strength with flowers!

The Pilgrim's wild and wintry day
Its shadow round us draws;
The Mayflower of his stormy bay,
Our Freedom's struggling cause.

But warmer suns erelong shall bring
To life the frozen sod;
And through dead leaves of hope shall spring
Afresh the flowers of God!

## THE LAST WALK IN AUTUMN.

### I.

O'er the bare woods, whose outstretched hands
Plead with the leaden heavens in vain,
I see, beyond the valley lands,
The sea's long level dim with rain.
Around me all things, stark and dumb,
Seem praying for the snows to come,
And, for the summer bloom and greenness gone,
With winter's sunset lights and dazzling morn atone.

### II.

Along the river's summer walk,
The withered tufts of asters nod;
And trembles on its arid stalk
The boar plume of the goldenrod.
And on a ground of sombre fir,
And azurestudded juniper,

The silver birch its buds of purple shows,
And scarlet berries tell where bloomed the sweet wildrose!

### III.

With mingled sound of horns and bells,
A farheard clang, the wild geese fly,
Stormsent, from Arctic moors and fells,
Like a great arrow through the sky,
Two dusky lines converged in one,
Chasing the southwardflying sun;
While the brave snowbird and the hardy jay
Call to them from the pines, as if to bid them stay.

### IV.

I passed this way a year ago
The wind blew south; the noon of day
Was warm as June's; and save that snow
Flecked the low mountains far away,
And that the vernalseeming breeze
Mocked faded grass and leafless trees,
I might have dreamed of summer as I lay,
Watching the fallen leaves with the soft wind at play.

### V.

Since then, the winter blasts have piled
The white pagodas of the snow
On these rough slopes, and, strong and wild,
Yon river, in its overflow
Of springtime rain and sun, set free,
Crashed with its ices to the sea;
And over these gray fields, then green and gold,
The summer corn has waved, the thunder's organ rolled.

### VI.

Rich gift of God! A year of time
What pomp of rise and shut of day,
What hues wherewith our Northern clime

Makes autumn's dropping woodlands gay,
What airs outblown from ferny dells,
And cloverbloom and sweetbrier smells,
What songs of brooks and birds, what fruits and flowers,
Green woods and moonlit snows, have in its round been ours!

## VII.

I know not how, in other lands,
The changing seasons come and go;
What splendors fall on Syrian sands,
What purple lights on Alpine snow!
Nor how the pomp of sunrise waits
On Venice at her watery gates;
A dream alone to me is Arno's vale,
And the Alhambra's halls are but a traveller's tale.

## VIII.

Yet, on life's current, he who drifts
Is one with him who rows or sails
And he who wanders widest lifts
No more of beauty's jealous veils
Than he who from his doorway sees
The miracle of flowers and trees,
Feels the warm Orient in the noonday air,
And from cloud minarets hears the sunset call to prayer!

## IX.

The eye may well be glad that looks
Where Pharpar's fountains rise and fall;
But he who sees his native brooks
Laugh in the sun, has seen them all.
The marble palaces of Ind
Rise round him in the snow and wind;
From his lone sweetbrier Persian Hafiz smiles,
And Rome's cathedral awe is in his woodland aisles.

## X.

And thus it is my fancy blends
The near at hand and far and rare;
And while the same horizon bends
Above the silversprinkled hair
Which flashed the light of morning skies
On childhood's wonderlifted eyes,
Within its round of sea and sky and field,
Earth wheels with all her zones, the Kosmos stands revealed.

## XI.

And thus the sick man on his bed,
The toiler to his taskwork bound,
Behold their prisonwalls outspread,
Their clipped horizon widen round!
While freedomgiving fancy waits,
Like Peter's angel at the gates,
The power is theirs to baffle care and pain,
To bring the lost world back, and make it theirs again!

## XII.

What lack of goodly company,
When masters of the ancient lyre
Obey my call, and trace for me
Their words of mingled tears and fire!
I talk with Bacon, grave and wise,
I read the world with Pascal's eyes;
And priest and sage, with solemn brows austere,
And poets, garlandbound, the Lords of Thought, draw near.

## XIII.

Methinks, O friend, I hear thee say,
"In vain the human heart we mock;
Bring living guests who love the day,
Not ghosts who fly at crow of cock!
The herbs we share with flesh and blood
Are better than ambrosial food

With laurelled shades." I grant it, nothing loath,
But doubly blest is he who can partake of both.

### XIV.

He who might Plato's banquet grace,
Have I not seen before me sit,
And watched his puritanic face,
With more than Eastern wisdom lit?
Shrewd mystic! who, upon the back
Of his Poor Richard's Almanac,
Writing the Sufi's song, the Gentoo's dream,
Links Manu's age of thought to Fulton's age of steam!

### XV.

Here too, of answering love secure,
Have I not welcomed to my hearth
The gentle pilgrim troubadour,
Whose songs have girdled half the earth;
Whose pages, like the magic mat
Whereon the Eastern lover sat,
Have borne me over Rhineland's purple vines,
And Nubia's tawny sands, and Phrygia's mountain pines!

### XVI.

And he, who to the lettered wealth
Of ages adds the lore unpriced,
The wisdom and the moral health,
The ethics of the school of Christ;
The statesman to his holy trust,
As the Athenian archon, just,
Struck down, exiled like him for truth alone,
Has he not graced my home with beauty all his own?

### XVII.

What greetings smile, what farewells wave,
What loved ones enter and depart!
The good, the beautiful, the brave,

The Heavenlent treasures of the heart!
How conscious seems the frozen sod
And beechen slope whereon they trod
The oakleaves rustle, and the dry grass bends
Beneath the shadowy feet of lost or absent friends.

## XVIII.

Then ask not why to these bleak hills
I cling, as clings the tufted moss,
To bear the winter's lingering chills,
The mocking spring's perpetual loss.
I dream of lands where summer smiles,
And soft winds blow from spicy isles,
But scarce would Ceylon's breath of flowers be sweet,
Could I not feel thy soil, New England, at my feet!

## XIX.

At times I long for gentler skies,
And bathe in dreams of softer air,
But homesick tears would fill the eyes
That saw the Cross without the Bear.
The pine must whisper to the palm,
The northwind break the tropic calm;
And with the dreamy languor of the Line,
The North's keen virtue blend, and strength to beauty join.

## XX.

Better to stem with heart and hand
The roaring tide of life, than lie,
Unmindful, on its flowery strand,
Of God's occasions drifting by
Better with naked nerve to bear
The needles of this goading air,
Than, in the lap of sensual ease, forego
The godlike power to do, the godlike aim to know.

## XXI.

Home of my heart! to me more fair
Than gay Versailles or Windsor's halls,
The painted, shingly townhouse where
The freeman's vote for Freedom falls!
The simple roof where prayer is made,
Than Gothic groin and colonnade;
The living temple of the heart of man,
Than Rome's skymocking vault, or manyspired Milan!

### XXII.

More dear thy equal village schools,
Where rich and poor the Bible read,
Than classic halls where Priestcraft rules,
And Learning wears the chains of Creed;
Thy glad Thanksgiving, gathering in
The scattered sheaves of home and kin,
Than the mad license ushering Lenten pains,
Or holidays of slaves who laugh and dance in chains.

### XXIII.

And sweet homes nestle in these dales,
And perch along these wooded swells;
And, blest beyond Arcadian vales,
They hear the sound of Sabbath bells!
Here dwells no perfect man sublime,
Nor woman winged before her time,
But with the faults and follies of the race,
Old homebred virtues hold their not unhonored place.

### XXIV.

Here manhood struggles for the sake
Of mother, sister, daughter, wife,
The graces and the loves which make
The music of the march of life;
And woman, in her daily round
Of duty, walks on holy ground.
No unpaid menial tills the soil, nor here
Is the bad lesson learned at human rights to sneer.

## XXV.

Then let the icy northwind blow
The trumpets of the coming storm,
To arrowy sleet and blinding snow
Yon slanting lines of rain transform.
Young hearts shall hail the drifted cold,
As gayly as I did of old;
And I, who watch them through the frosty pane,
Unenvious, live in them my boyhood o'er again.

## XXVI.

And I will trust that He who heeds
The life that hides in mead and wold,
Who hangs yon alder's crimson beads,
And stains these mosses green and gold,
Will still, as He hath done, incline
His gracious care to me and mine;
Grant what we ask aright, from wrong debar,
And, as the earth grows dark, make brighter every star!

## XXVII.

I have not seen, I may not see,
My hopes for man take form in fact,
But God will give the victory
In due time; in that faith I act.
And lie who sees the future sure,
The baffling present may endure,
And bless, meanwhile, the unseen Hand that leads
The heart's desires beyond the halting step of deeds.

## XXVIII.

And thou, my song, I send thee forth,
Where harsher songs of mine have flown;
Go, find a place at home and hearth
Where'er thy singer's name is known;
Revive for him the kindly thought
Of friends; and they who love him not,

Touched by some strain of thine, perchance may take
The hand he proffers all, and thank him for thy sake.

## THE FIRST FLOWERS

For ages on our river borders,
These tassels in their tawny bloom,
And willowy studs of downy silver,
Have prophesied of Spring to come.

For ages have the unbound waters
Smiled on them from their pebbly hem,
And the clear carol of the robin
And song of bluebird welcomed them.

But never yet from smiling river,
Or song of early bird, have they
Been greeted with a gladder welcome
Than whispers from my heart today.

They break the spell of cold and darkness,
The weary watch of sleepless pain;
And from my heart, as from the river,
The ice of winter melts again.

Thanks, Mary! for this wildwood token
Of Freya's footsteps drawing near;
Almost, as in the rune of Asgard,
The growing of the grass I hear.

It is as if the pinetrees called me
From ceiled room and silent books,
To see the dance of woodland shadows,
And hear the song of April brooks!

As in the old Teutonic ballad
Of Odenwald live bird and tree,
Together live in bloom and music,
I blend in song thy flowers and thee.

Earth's rocky tablets bear forever

The dint of rain and small bird's track
Who knows but that my idle verses
May leave some trace by Merrimac!

The bird that trod the mellow layers
Of the young earth is sought in vain;
The cloud is gone that wove the sandstone,
From God's design, with threads of rain!

So, when this fluid age we live in
Shall stiffen round my careless rhyme,
Who made the vagrant tracks may puzzle
The savants of the coming time;

And, following out their dim suggestions,
Some idlycurious hand may draw
My doubtful portraiture, as Cuvier
Drew fish and bird from fin and claw.

And maidens in the faroff twilights,
Singing my words to breeze and stream,
Shall wonder if the oldtime Mary
Were real, or the rhymer's dream!

## THE OLD BURYINGGROUND.

Our vales are sweet with fern and rose,
Our hills are maplecrowned;
But not from them our fathers chose
The village buryingground.

The dreariest spot in all the land
To Death they set apart;
With scanty grace from Nature's hand,
And none from that of Art.

A winding wall of mossy stone,
Frostflung and broken, lines
A lonesome acre thinly grown
With grass and wandering vines.

Without the wall a birchtree shows
Its drooped and tasselled head;
Within, a staghorned sumach grows,
Fernleafed, with spikes of red.

There, sheep that graze the neighboring plain
Like white ghosts come and go,
The farmhorse drags his fetlock chain,
The cowbell tinkles slow.

Low moans the river from its bed,
The distant pines reply;
Like mourners shrinking from the dead,
They stand apart and sigh.

Unshaded smites the summer sun,
Unchecked the winter blast;
The schoolgirl learns the place to shun,
With glances backward cast.

For thus our fathers testified,
That he might read who ran,
The emptiness of human pride,
The nothingness of man.

They dared not plant the grave with flowers,
Nor dress the funeral sod,
Where, with a love as deep as ours,
They left their dead with God.

The hard and thorny path they kept
From beauty turned aside;
Nor missed they over those who slept
The grace to life denied.

Yet still the wilding flowers would blow,
The golden leaves would fall,
The seasons come, the seasons go,
And God be good to all.

Above the graves the' blackberry hung

In bloom and green its wreath,
And harebells swung as if they rung
The chimes of peace beneath.

The beauty Nature loves to share,
The gifts she hath for all,
The common light, the common air,
O'ercrept the graveyard's wall.

It knew the glow of eventide,
The sunrise and the noon,
And glorified and sanctified
It slept beneath the moon.

With flowers or snowflakes for its sod,
Around the seasons ran,
And evermore the love of God
Rebuked the fear of man.

We dwell with fears on either hand,
Within a daily strife,
And spectral problems waiting stand
Before the gates of life.

The doubts we vainly seek to solve,
The truths we know, are one;
The known and nameless stars revolve
Around the Central Sun.

And if we reap as we have sown,
And take the dole we deal,
The law of pain is love alone,
The wounding is to heal.

Unharmed from change to change we glide,
We fall as in our dreams;
The faroff terror at our side
A smiling angel seems.

Secure on God's alltender heart
Alike rest great and small;

Why fear to lose our little part,
When He is pledged for all?

O fearful heart and troubled brain
Take hope and strength from this,
That Nature never hints in vain,
Nor prophesies amiss.

Her wild birds sing the same sweet stave,
Her lights and airs are given
Alike to playground and the grave;
And over both is Heaven.

## THE PALMTREE.

Is it the palm, the cocoapalm,
On the Indian Sea, by the isles of balm?
Or is it a ship in the breezeless calm?

A ship whose keel is of palm beneath,
Whose ribs of palm have a palmbark sheath,
And a rudder of palm it steereth with.

Branches of palm are its spars and rails,
Fibres of palm are its woven sails,
And the rope is of palm that idly trails!

What does the good ship bear so well?
The cocoanut with its stony shell,
And the milky sap of its inner cell.

What are its jars, so smooth and fine,
But hollowed nuts, filled with oil and wine,
And the cabbage that ripens under the Line?

Who smokes his nargileh, cool and calm?
The master, whose cunning and skill could charm
Cargo and ship from the bounteous palm.

In the cabin he sits on a palmmat soft,
From a beaker of palm his drink is quaffed,

And a palmthatch shields from the sun aloft!

His dress is woven of palmy strands,
And he holds a palmleaf scroll in his hands,
Traced with the Prophet's wise commands!

The turban folded about his head
Was daintily wrought of the palmleaf braid,
And the fan that cools him of palm was made.

Of threads of palm was the carpet spun
Whereon he kneels when the day is done,
And the foreheads of Islam are bowed as one!

To him the palm is a gift divine,
Wherein all uses of man combine,
House, and raiment, and food, and wine!

And, in the hour of his great release,
His need of the palm shall only cease
With the shroud wherein he lieth in peace.

"Allah il Allah!" he sings his psalm,
On the Indian Sea, by the isles of balm;
"Thanks to Allah who gives the palm!

## THE RIVER PATH.

No birdsong floated down the hill,
The tangled bank below was still;

No rustle from the birchen stem,
No ripple from the water's hem.

The dusk of twilight round us grew,
We felt the falling of the dew;

For, from us, ere the day was done,
The wooded hills shut out the sun.

But on the river's farther side

We saw the hilltops glorified,

A tender glow, exceeding fair,
A dream of day without its glare.

With us the damp, the chill, the gloom
With them the sunset's rosy bloom;

While dark, through willowy vistas seen,
The river rolled in shade between.

From out the darkness where we trod,
We gazed upon those bills of God,

Whose light seemed not of moon or sun.
We spake not, but our thought was one.

We paused, as if from that bright shore
Beckoned our dear ones gone before;

And stilled our beating hearts to hear
The voices lost to mortal ear!

Sudden our pathway turned from night;
The hills swung open to the light;

Through their green gates the sunshine showed,
A long, slant splendor downward flowed.

Down glade and glen and bank it rolled;
It bridged the shaded stream with gold;

And, borne on piers of mist, allied
The shadowy with the sunlit side!

"So," prayed we, "when our feet draw near
The river dark, with mortal fear,

"And the night cometh chill with dew,
O Father! let Thy light break through!

"So let the hills of doubt divide,
So bridge with faith the sunless tide!

"So let the eyes that fail on earth
On Thy eternal hills look forth;

"And in Thy beckoning angels know
The dear ones whom we loved below!"

## MOUNTAIN PICTURES.

### I. FRANCONIA FROM THE PEMIGEWASSET

Once more, O Mountains of the North, unveil
Your brows, and lay your cloudy mantles by
And once more, ere the eyes that seek ye fail,
Uplift against the blue walls of the sky

Your mighty shapes, and let the sunshine weave
Its golden network in your belting woods,
Smile down in rainbows from your falling floods,
And on your kingly brows at morn and eve
Set crowns of fire! So shall my soul receive

Haply the secret of your calm and strength,
Your unforgotten beauty interfuse

My common life, your glorious shapes and hues
And sundropped splendors at my bidding come,
Loom vast through dreams, and stretch in billowy length
From the sealevel of my lowland home!

They rise before me! Last night's thundergust
Roared not in vain: for where its lightnings thrust
Their tongues of fire, the great peaks seem so near,
Burned clean of mist, so starkly bold and clear,
I almost pause the wind in the pines to hear,

The loose rock's fall, the steps of browsing deer.
The clouds that shattered on yon slideworn walls
And splintered on the rocks their spears of rain

Have set in play a thousand waterfalls,
Making the dusk and silence of the woods
Glad with the laughter of the chasing floods,
And luminous with blown spray and silver gleams,
While, in the vales below, the drylipped streams
Sing to the freshened meadowlands again.

So, let me hope, the battlestorm that beats
The land with hail and fire may pass away
With its spent thunders at the break of day,
Like last night's clouds, and leave, as it retreats,
A greener earth and fairer sky behind,
Blown crystalclear by Freedom's Northern wind!

## II. MONADNOCK FROM WACHUSET.

I would I were a painter, for the sake
Of a sweet picture, and of her who led,
A fitting guide, with reverential tread,
Into that mountain mystery. First a lake
Tinted with sunset; next the wavy lines
Of far receding hills; and yet more far,

Monadnock lifting from his night of pines
His rosy forehead to the evening star.
Beside us, purplezoned, Wachuset laid

His head against the West, whose warm light made
His aureole; and o'er him, sharp and clear,
Like a shaft of lightning in midlaunching stayed,
A single level cloudline, shone upon

By the fierce glances of the sunken sun,
Menaced the darkness with its golden spear!

So twilight deepened round us. Still and black
The great woods climbed the mountain at our back;
And on their skirts, where yet the lingering day
On the shorn greenness of the clearing lay,

The brown old farmhouse like a bird'snest hung.
With homelife sounds the desert air was stirred
The bleat of sheep along the hill we heard,
The bucket plashing in the cool, sweet well,
The pasturebars that clattered as they fell;

Dogs barked, fowls fluttered, cattle lowed; the gate
Of the barnyard creaked beneath the merry weight
Of sunbrown children, listening, while they swung,
The welcome sound of suppercall to hear;

And down the shadowy lane, in tinklings clear,
The pastoral curfew of the cowbell rung.
Thus soothed and pleased, our backward path we took,
Praising the farmer's home. He only spake,

Looking into the sunset o'er the lake,

Like one to whom the faroff is most near:
"Yes, most folks think it has a pleasant look;
I love it for my good old mother's sake,

Who lived and died here in the peace of God!"
The lesson of his words we pondered o'er,
As silently we turned the eastern flank

Of the mountain, where its shadow deepest sank,
Doubling the night along our rugged road:
We felt that man was more than his abode,
The inward life than Nature's raiment more;
And the warm sky, the sundowntinted hill,

The forest and the lake, seemed dwarfed and dim
Before the saintly soul, whose human will
Meekly in the Eternal footsteps trod,

Making her homely toil and household ways
An earthly echo of the song of praise
Swelling from angel lips and harps of seraphim.

www.ingramcontent.com/pod-product-compliance
Lightning Source LLC
Chambersburg PA
CBHW081733100526
44591CB00016B/2600